The Show Must Go On
A Journey Through Life in Poetry

by Lisa Ventura MBE

With Guest Contributions From

Suz Winspear
Mel Scott
Giovanni "Spoz" Esposito

Lisa Ventura MBE

Unity Group Solutions Limited, The Oakley, Kidderminster Road, Droitwich, Worcestershire, United Kingdom, WR9 9AY
Tel: 0800 772 0155
Email: info@csu.org.uk
Web: www.csu.org.uk

ISBN: 978-1-326-56516-9

Dedication, Acknowledgements, and Thanks

My sincere thanks go to everyone over my lifetime who has and continues to support me, champion me and helped me to succeed, it means more to me than you will ever know. This book is dedicated to you all.

I also dedicate this book and thank my wonderful husband Russell Ventura for his unwavering support in everything I do and for putting up with me despite being so neurodivergent (diagnosed with autism, ADHD, dyspraxia, and dyscalculia). I know how challenging that is to deal with, and you are the John to my Kayleigh always (see what I'm doing, see what I'm doing) 8-) ♡♡

This collection is also dedicated to Leena Batchelor, Dan and Rhianna Levi-Burton and Script Haven, Worcester's finest independent book and coffee shop, without whom I would never have got my "mojo" back for creative writing and poetry.

And finally, a big thank you goes to all my amazing Facebook friends who helped me to come up with a title for this poetry collection. As a huge fan of the rock band Queen and Freddie Mercury, "The Show Must Go On" was a very apt and fitting title. I thank you all from the bottom of my heart.

This collection is also dedicated to Leena Batchelor, Dan and Rhianna Levi-Burton and Script Haven, Worcester's finest independent book and coffee shop, without whom I would never have got my "mojo back for creative writing and poetry":

I would never have got this book out for its launch date of 3 April

Dedication, Acknowledgements, and Thanks

2025 without James Bore of Security Blend Books, my publisher for the "Rise of the Cyber Women" and "Varied Origins of the Cyber Men" book series that I launched in 2020. While I knew it was not appropriate for this book to be released via Security Blend Books, my thanks go to James for his help and input with typesetting and preparing the book for release on a platform away from Amazon Direct Publishing.

Contents

CONTENTS

CONTENTS

CONTENTS

Introduction

My name is Lisa Ventura MBE, and I am most known for the award-winning work I do in the cyber security industry and in artificial intelligence (AI), not just in the UK but globally. In 2009 I pivoted into the cyber security industry after working with Chris Tarrant of "Who Wants to be a Millionaire" fame for many years, and I never looked back. I was also the Founder and Director of the first ever literary festival in my area, the Worcestershire Literary Festival, which I launched in 2011. I intended for the festival to just take place in Worcester, but due to the massive amount of interest it had, it ended up running over 10 days with over 130 events across the entire county of Worcestershire.

Why did I launch a festival of that magnitude? I did it because ever since I was old enough to pick up a pen and put it to paper, writing has been my thing, my "special interest" if you like, especially creative writing including poetry, short stories and fiction writing. In 2013 I had to deal with an incredibly upsetting incident of bullying and abuse, as well as a personal tragedy that I thought I would never recover from (more on this later), and I lost my "mojo" for creative writing completely. I was DONE with it.

Since I had to pick myself up and dust myself off in 2013 after that, I launched the UK's first ever trade association in cyber security, the UK Cyber Security Association. I've launched the Unity Group which includes Cyber Security Unity, AI Unity and Neuro Unity. At the age of 45 I discovered that I am neurodivergent (diagnosed with autism, ADHD, dyspraxia and dyscalculia) and realised this is why I have struggled so much in my life. Through this, I also do a lot of work in the diversity, equity, belonging and inclusion space.

I've also endured a significant amount of bullying and abuse in every area of my life from as far back as I can remember, sometimes from the very people who should have loved me and accepted me unconditionally. Despite this, I've motored on with my career and I've been shortlisted for, been a finalist for and won numerous awards for my work, but the proudest moment of my life was being presented with an MBE by King Charles III for services to cyber security and diversity, equity, belonging and inclusion. It was a massive "f**k you" moment to each and every person who had ever bullied and abused me in my lifetime – and there have been many! It also proved that I am enough. I was always enough; despite what the bullies and abusers would have me believe.

I've also been through some very significant trauma in my lifetime, the main trauma experience being when I lost my only son Francesco "Frankie" Enrico Ventura to stillbirth on 29 November 2013. There were times in my life when I was suicidal because of things that happened to me and the way I had been treated by bullies and abusers. In the end I went no contact with them all, and although it was very hard at the time, life got so much better as a result.

Through all this poetry has always been a sanctuary for me - a place where I can express my deepest emotions, capture fleeting moments, and make sense of the world around me. It has been my companion through joy and sorrow, through triumph and adversity. This collection, *The Show Must Go On*, is a deeply personal journey, told through verse, of the highs and lows, the laughter and tears, the real-life observations I've made and the resilience that has shaped my life.

This poetry collection is not just my voice; it is a chorus of experiences. I am honoured to include contributions from Giovanni "Spoz" Esposito, Suz Winspear, and Mel Scott – all very remarkable poets who bring their own unique perspectives and powerful words to these pages. Their poetry enriches this collection, creating a tapestry of stories that resonate with love, loss, and the unwavering human spirit.

The title *The Show Must Go On* was inspired by one of my greatest musical influences, the rock band Queen and Freddie Mercury. It is a fitting tribute to the perseverance and strength that life demands of us. No matter what challenges we face, no matter the heartbreaks we endure, we must keep moving forward, even if there are times when we feel we can't. Life, like poetry, is a performance - one that demands courage, passion, and above all, authenticity.

Through my poems you will find themes of love, loss, hope, resilience, and the ever-evolving journey of self-discovery. From reflections on my personal struggles to observations about the world around me, I hope that my words, and those of my fellow contributors, offer comfort, inspiration, and perhaps even a little light humour.

To all those who have supported me, encouraged me, and walked this journey with me - this poetry collection is for you. And to every reader who finds solace in poetry, may these words remind you that no matter what happens, *the show must go on.*

Love and hugs,

Lisa Ventura MBE April 2025

Worcestershire Literary Festival

In 2011 I founded the Worcestershire Literary Festival which took place throughout the whole County. It was meant to be quite small scale to start with and based just in the city of Worcester, but the interest from all over Worcestershire was such that it quickly grew and became the Worcestershire Literary Festival with over 130 events over 10 days in June 2011 – I definitely don't do things by halves!

I wrote this poem at the time to mark the launch of the first festival:

I'm a poet, I love literature, and I love to read and write
So in 2011 decided to put a festival in my sight
The Worcestershire Literary Festival was born
With talks, book signings, poetry slams and events galore

June 14 to 23 are the dates
When the festival runs, so come along with your mates
A Poet Laureate for Worcestershire we seek
Who will be our new bard... if it is not too much of a
cheek!

This festival is for YOU, and it is all over the Shire
Hopefully you won't think it is too dire
Pop me a message if you want to find out more
And like your favourite sports team, I hope this festival
will score!

Guest Poem - Sleep Should be a Forest

by Suz Winspear

Sleep should be a forest, not a desert –
no lost and waste expanse of empty time
spread on blank and icy fitted sheets,
unfilled, unwanted, always profitless,
useless hours before the clock's alarm
awakes the world's activities again.

No, sleep should be a forest,
endless, dark and deep,
a place to curl among
the time-worn trunks of ancient trees
rich with scents of fallen leaves' decay,
to hear the living rustling sounds
of insects moving in the loam beneath,
and birdsong voices all around.
Hear the songs they sing you as you curl
deeper down into the forest floor,
connecting, ever re-connecting
with the old instinctive dance of life,
here where you can taste
the water of the enigmatic spring
where the longest darkest ash tree root
reaches down, far down, to catch the essence
of the truest world that waits
beyond the waking times,
deeper than the morning's glare,
the harsh and hateful urgency of ticking clocks.

Guest Poem - After the Storm

by Suz Winspear

The storm was raging overnight.
This morning there's no need to get up early -
the trains aren't running anyway.
Let's have breakfast, take our time –
things won't be getting any worse.

Let's pause for a bit.

Fallen trees will still be fallen later,
they don't require immediate attention.
Later, the garden fence can be repaired,
appointments made for tiles to be replaced,
the shed can be retrieved from the canal.
Later will be chainsaw-time.
But now we have a clear-skied dawn,
strong hot tea is in the pot
and melting butter sparkles in the frying pan.

About Suz Winspear

*Suz Winspear is a poet, writer, and performer known for her vivid,
imaginative poetry that explores themes of gothic beauty, the supernat-
ural, and the human condition. Her work often blends dark humour
with striking imagery, reflecting her fascination with history, mythol-
ogy, and the macabre. Suz has been a key figure in the Worcestershire*

poetry scene and served as the Poet Laureate of Worcestershire from 2016 to 2017. A dynamic performer, she brings her poetry to life on stage with theatrical flair, captivating audiences with her distinctive voice and storytelling style.

Keith the Worcestershire Seal

In 2013 a seal was spotted in the River Severn by the Ketch Caravan Park and was affectionately named by locals as Keith after a Royalist Commander in the English Civil War. However, it turned out that "he" was a "she".

The Angling Trust wanted to shoot her as they feared she was eating all the fish reserves in the river, so I started a campaign called #SaveKeith. It went viral and was picked up not just in the local press but in all the national press, and even by some international news outlets.

I wrote this poem in 2013 when Keith the Worcestershire Seal went viral:

Photo by Dave Grubb

It appeared one day completely out of the blue
It was floating on its back, enjoying the view
People couldn't believe the sight that met their eyes
A seal in the river, now that was a surprise!

It was named Keith after a Royalist Commander
In the English Civil War, but that was a blinder
Keith it turned out was a girl you see
And not a boy after all, glory be!

She took up residence in the Severn and hedged her bets
She was seen in a caravan park up by the Ketch
Everyone wanted to see Keith the seal
They looked at the river anxiously with excitement and zeal

She was seen in Bewdley, Upton, Worcester and Stourport
All over Worcestershire she was caught
On camera and film, nothing less
She was even featured in the national press

Then a girl called Coco caught Keith on the hop
While she was having a fish snack, it was a fair cop
The footage was picked up by the BBC
And was broadcast to the region for all to see

Then the Angling Trust got on their high horse
Keith would eat all the fish they said, she would show no remorse
They would shoot Keith if she didn't go back to sea
They wouldn't just let her be

I launched a petition against this cruel threat
Over 3000 people signed it, unprepared to bet
That the Angling Trust would be so cruel
But in the end, the Angling Trust were the fools

Keith now has her own Facebook page
With nearly 4000 fans, she must be in quite a daze
She become quite a local celebrity
Everyone wanted a glimpse of Keith, she is sure to be

A legend of Worcestershire and a symbol of fun
A tale to tell our children, of when we saw Keith in the sun
Lying on her back with her flippers in the air
Enjoying her new habitat without a care

Please spare a thought for our seal
She captured our hearts and was the real deal
Keith you're a star, thank you for brightening our day
Please stay in the Severn, come what may

Dear Mr Mark Zuckerberg

I wrote this poem in 2011 when Mark Zuckerberg, the Creator of Facebook, announced that the platform would move to a new and unwelcome feature – the timeline.

Dear Mr Mark Zukerberg
Why do you want to change Facebook again?
Have you not heard the saying "if it ain't broke don't
fix it"?
It really is quite a pain

You are forcing the timeline upon us
Telling us it is for our own good
So why does my Facebook have to change
Just because you think it should?

You are the king of social networking
They even made a film about you
You think it is OK to mess with the timeline
And change how Facebook looks as if on cue

But these latest changes are beyond a joke
It really does beggar belief
We have to relearn how to use it
These changes are not welcome, they fill me with such
grief!

But soon you say it will be D-day
And Facebook will change yet again
And I will have no choice in the matter
These constant changes are driving me insane

We are all addicted to Facebook
When our phones beep we jump
To see what status updates await us from our friends
On a new look Facebook page that is about as welcome
      as a lump

I could just delete my account
And not use Facebook again
But the reality is you have "Zuckered" us all in
I would lose much more than I would gain

So Dear Mr Mark Zuckerberg
I hope you understand when I say
The timeline is very unwelcome
And I wish it would just go away!

Ode to Jeremy Clarkson or... And Another Thing!

I wrote this poem in 2015 when Jeremy Clarkson punched a co-worker and was sacked from Top Gear and the BBC. At the time I wasn't a huge fan of his, but he has grown on me in recent years because of "The Grand Tour" and especially because of "Clarkson's Farm".

His day of reckoning is finally here
The old dinosaur has a lot to fear
His contract has been terminated by the BBC
No more Clarkson on there for you and me

Jeremy has finally bitten the dust
He punched a co-worker, and therefore he must
Pay the price for his actions and oafish behaviour
No longer is he a UK saviour

I love Top Gear, it has to be said
But I'm sure it will go on with another presenter instead
My money is on Chris Evans of Radio 2
He'd be a great replacement, his time is due

So bye bye Jeremy, you have a long time to think
About the consequences of your actions, because they

stink
You overstepped the mark, you crossed the line
But I'm sure Top Gear will be totally fine

The Hamster and May will be better off
Without this big-headed arrogant toff
Jeremy Clarkson, your time is finally up at last
How does it feel to be a thing of the past?

9/11 Terror

In September 2001 I wrote two poems when the horrific attack on the World Trade Centre and the Pentagon happened, I couldn't get my head around what happened and still haven't to this day.

This is the first poem I wrote.

A bright day dawned that September morn
The sky was clear and blue, a new day was born
New York awoke and came to life
No indication of the pending destruction and strife

Mums and dads, sons and daughter's brothers and sisters
Friends and neighbours went off to work
Every person special, every person so loved
The murder of each one leaves us so bereaved

They went into that snare, an unexpected trap
No warning, no chance no way out but death
For thousands there was no escape
A violent death, recorded on tape.

We cannot begin to imagine the terror the hostages went through
The realisation that their death was so near
Their hearts and minds filled with fear
A last phone call to their loved ones
A message of love was the last they would send
The plane turned bomb took them to their terrible end

A terror came out of the skies
Those innocent victims, the terrorists ignored their cries
A speed of 500 miles an hour
The plane deliberately ploughed into the tower
Shock, horror and disbelief
America could not hide its grief
Some lucky ones escaped with their life
Some so badly burned, injured but alive
They ran and fled as fast as they were able
But the unthinkable happened, the tower fell
The consequence was a living hell

Shards of glass and hot molten metal
Cut into our precious people
Severing the bodies into pieces
Burning them to ashes

Not many have been found
Lost forever on the mound
No body to bury, no funeral to have
No proper goodbye to the end of each life

Eleven acres of destruction now called ground zero
Each volunteer was hailed as a hero
The terrible chaos and desolation of that site
Those wonderful twin towers brought down from their great height

Shock waves went out all over the world
An act which will have to be solved
The world unites on this issue
We hope and pray war will not ensue

What has happened is beyond belief
How can we cope with our grief?
But the spirit of America will win through
The stars and stripes will fly high and true

Our freedom preserved; our minds free from terror
Our existence secure and our world free from horror

Osama Bin Laden? Osama Bin Laden????
But I've never heard of him. . .

9/11

Where were you on that fateful day?
Were you at work or at home, were you waiting for your
    pay?
Did you see the news, did you hear it on the wireless?
Did you stop and listen, or did you carry on regardless?

The day was a day just like any other
Work, bills – oh I and I must visit my mother!
So much to do and very little time
To not complete everything would have been a crime

I returned from lunch and got on with my day
Unaware things would change in such a dramatic way
Someone came into my office, in a bit of a state
A plane had crashed in New York, he said, I can't get
    hold of my mate

We all gathered around the TV in horror and shock
This was certainly no time to mock
The twin towers of New York were there, tall and true
And the sky surrounding them was a deep shade of blue

But embedded in one of the towers was a passenger plane
Surrounded by smoke and big giant flame
This must be an accident, this must be a mistake
Then a second plane appeared and I began to quake

On the TV images were beamed live with such power
A second plane then appeared and struck the other tower
This was no accident, this was no mistake
America was under attack, many lives were at stake

The fire burnt brighter against the blue of the sky
The way of life as we knew it had to die
People were trapped and couldn't break free
Mothers, fathers, sons, daughters. . . .they would not ever
    see

Their loved ones again, it was so very sad
They tried to call, to say I love you Dad
Then something terrible happened
The towers collapsed, and everything silenced

Let's take a moment to think and reflect
To remember those involved, the lives lost and the dead
Today it is called Ground Zero
Buried below are hundreds of souls, every one of them a
    hero

A beautiful memorial garden now stands in their place
A new tower is being built to represent freedom and grace
Trees adorn where the towers once stood tall and true
This memorial site gives hope to me and to you

Climate Change

I wrote this poem in 2011 for the "Earth Hour" event that was part of the Worcestershire Literary Festival and is now an annual event every March. Earth Hour has been known for the "lights off" moment, with individuals from around the globe switching off their lights to show symbolic support for the planet and to raise awareness of the environmental issues affecting it.

Trees, plants, flowers and grass bright green
They are out in full bloom, an amazing sight to be seen
Spring is almost behind us and Summer is getting near
It is now time to sit outside drinking beer

Our world is such a wondrous place
We have so much to behold, it is really rather....well, ace
We think we can do what we like to our land
But one day it could all turn to dust and sand

The world's resources are not finite
They are precious and we should conserve them with all our
        might
They will not be here forever and ever
But we think they will be – run out of oil and gas? No, never!

Why do we take the car everywhere?
Why don't we leave it at home and walk without a care?
Why don't we enjoy a brisk stroll getting fit?
What did we do before we did nothing but sit?

Climate change is our biggest threat
We ignore it at our peril, and are willing to bet
We must think of the future and generations to come
We must think of preserving our earth for us all, not just for
    some

We must show our children the beauty of life
We must help polar bears and the pandas survive this strife
No matter how old you are or that you may only be a teen
It's never too early or too late to be green

Ode to Dog Owners to be Responsible... or Please Pick Up Your Dog's Poo!

I wrote this in 2011 when I was incensed at the amount of dog poo I often encountered that hadn't been picked up by irresponsible dog owners when out walking with my dogs;

It only takes a minute
To pick up after your pooch
It keeps the environment clean and tidy
If they've been to the toilet while having a mooch

It is horrible if you step in dog mess
I know this to my cost
It is unpleasant and foul smelling
My shoes were thrown away and lost

There are bins strategically placed
For you to deposit their poo
Please use them when out walking
If your dog decides to go to the loo

Ode to Dog Owners to be Responsible...

Please be a responsible owner
Don't sit on the fence
Carry bags and pick up after your dog
As Del Boy from Only Fools & Horses says...you know
it make sense!

Follow Your Intuition

As someone who is neurodivergent, I have been the target of bullying and abuse that started as soon as I was born and carried on throughout every area of my life. My most recent experience of bullying and abuse was in the workplace at the age of 50, but I've had it from family, at school/college, from so-called friends and in the workplace.

I then became a specialist in narcissism and narcissistic personality disorder, and this poem came about after a very upsetting experience of bullying and abuse in 2013 when I was 5 months pregnant with my son Frankie who I lost to stillbirth:

> Follow your intuition
> It is usually always right
> Always follow your gut feelings
> And trust them with all your might
>
> Don't let negative people drag you down
> And paralyse your confidence and self-esteem
> And beware of the ones who talk badly of others
> They'll talk badly about you too, they are so mean
>
> These people are fly by night
> They go from pillar to post
> Looking for power, fame and glory
> They love themselves the most

So my advice to everyone
Is to surround yourself with those who care
Not with ones who are narcissistic and selfish
Who pull you into their poisoned lair

I've had my fill of drama queens, bullies and pompous
     twits
From now on I say no more!
I will trust my intuition implicitly
I don't care if that makes me a bore

If it doesn't feel right, I will walk away
Right at the very start
I don't care what anyone thinks
I will completely trust my heart

An Empty Armed Mother

On 29 November 2013 my life changed forever when my much loved and much wanted only son Francesco "Frankie" Enrico Ventura was born sleeping.

I wrote this poem at the time to try and get across how much pain I was in from his loss. It is followed by 2 poems from a very inspiring person in the baby loss community who helped me immensely at the time – Mel Scott, Found of "Towards Tomorrow Together."

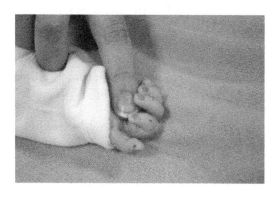

Am I or aren't I?
Am I a mother or not?
I DID give birth you see
But I have an empty cot....

I carried my son inside me
For 33 weeks I felt him grow
I couldn't wait for him to arrive
I loved him very much, this is so

All the things we would do together
I would sing him songs and read to him
I would tell him about sci-fi and Star Wars
I would always go out on a limb

To tell my son of the world we are in
And teach him to be good and kind
I wanted him to set an example
And grow up knowing his own mind

Instead.......

I am an empty armed mother
I am the one it happened to
No newborn to hold in my arms
No new life care for, it is true

I am one of the one in four
Who loses their babies before they are born
I am the one whose arms are empty
I am the one who feels torn

There were no children before my son
There have been none since he died
I am an empty armed mother
I have no children by my side

November 29

I wrote this poem in March 2014 when I was at the lowest point of my life after I lost my much loved and wanted son to stillbirth 3 months earlier in November 2013.

Is it March already?
I didn't realise....
I'm stuck in time
On November 29

My son was born sleeping that day
My heart was shattered and broken
It will never mend again
I feel like I'm going insane

All I want is to hold
My beautiful son in my arms
But grief consumes me
My loss so terribly plain to see

No newborn open eyes
No newborn smell
No newborn smiling or crying
If I said I was over it I'd be lying

People smile and laugh
They go along their way
I wasn't supposed to have this life
One without my son full of grief and strife

I was supposed to be a mother
Breastfeeding and changing nappies
Instead I have an empty nursery
With an empty cot as plain as can be

And no-one will ever know
My son who I held for a day
Who never smiled nor cried
But changed my life completely anyway

I cannot let your memory die
I cannot let your existence mean nothing
Your brief time on this earth will be
A wonderful thing through your legacy

So as each new day dawns
And the pain of losing you so raw
I will work hard day night and day
To raise awareness, come what may

Of cleft lip and palate
Of stillbirth and angels born sleeping
Of the rare chromosome disorder you had
That meant your life would be very very bad

Oh my sweet baby son Frankie
Do you know any different in heaven
What will I do without you
Do you know how much I miss you

Guest Poem - Mothering a Memory

by Mel Scott

I have an important job to do,
it's one that you can't see.
Most of the tasks are hidden from view,
I am mothering your memory.

I sit and chat or read to you,
alone in your nursery.
As I quietly hum your tune,
I am mothering your memory.

I walk to your grave to be with you,
Light the place that you're buried.
Sit in the early morning dew,
I am mothering your memory.

I take workers a cake or two,
warm a heart with my kind deeds.
Pay for someone's shopping in a queue,
I am mothering your memory.

As time goes on, I honour you,
and build you a legacy.
Through all the things that we choose,
I am mothering your memory.

We will always remember you -
share your name everywhere, Finley,
through all the things that we do.
I will always mother your memory.

Guest Poem - Still a Mum

by Mel Scott

Am I still a Mum,
if my baby doesn't move?
If family come to see us and
it's me they need to soothe.

Am I still a Mum,
if I didn't get them dressed?
If I couldn't feed them
from a bottle or my breast.

Am I still a Mum,
if I forgot their socks?
If I walked out of the hospital
carrying only a memory box?

Am I still a Mum,
if my baby didn't breathe?
If instead of feeling happy,
I live my life in grief.

Am I still a Mum,
if my baby didn't cry?
If I sit inside the nursery
on my own at night.

Am I still a Mum,
if my baby wasn't saved?
If instead of new-born gifts
I have to decorate their grave.

About Mel Scott

Mel Scott is an Occupational Therapist, doula and writer who experienced a miscarriage followed by the stillbirth of her son Finley. She first shared their story in her book Finley's Footprints, *and as inspiration for change through study days and events. Mel is founder of baby loss charity* Towards Tomorrow Together.

A Trail Called Hope... in memory of Enzo Simone

In 2011 I travelled to New York with my ex-wife Amy, and while there we met her cousin Enzo Simone. I got on with Enzo from the moment I met him, but sadly he passed away in 2020. The legacy he left behind as an advocate and awareness raiser for Alzheimer's Disease and Parkinson's Disease was incredible, as Enzo's mother Josie succumbed to Alzheimer's and his father-in-law succumbed to Parkinson's. I wrote this poem for Enzo:

> A quest for a cure
> A cure for two evil diseases
> Do you think you can't do anything?
> Do you think you can't help?
>
> Do you think it will never happen to you or anyone you
>   know?
> Are you blissfully unaware as they forget the smallest of
>   things?
> Do you not notice when their memory leaves them or their
>   body starts to shake?
> You shake your head, but not from illness. From denial.
>
> A husband whose wife has forgotten who she is
> A family torn apart by this awful disease and laid asunder

A son who wants to find a cure for Alzheimer's
This is his dream, a dream he cannot ever give up

Ten mountains to be climbed over ten years
His team called "the regulars" step up to the challenge
They climb Mount Blanc and Kilimanjaro
To raise awareness and money for much needed research

Even if you can't climb mountains you can still help
Give them your support, write them a letter
Help them to keep going against all the odds
Give them the strength to carry on

A quest for a cure
For two evil diseases
Alzheimer's and Parkinson's
A Trail Called Hope....

.....never give up that hope.

World up to all the regulars....always.

Age 50

On 14 October 2023 I turned 50 years old, and to mark the occasion of having lived on this earth for half a century (an incredible achievement when many others I know didn't get that far), I wrote this poem:

Age 50 - what does it mean?
It means I am the same as I've always been
I'm the same size now as when I was sixteen
I will never be a has been!

I'm still something of a gem
I can still wear short skirts with the best of them
My legs are slim and still look good
I could pull a guy half my age if I thought I would

I can party and dance all night
I don't need Ecstasy to get as high as a kite
Life is fast and exciting
Life is for living not contemplating

I live life loud with heavy metal
Ozzy rules - like me he'll never settle
Live life in the fast lane is my way
I'll never get old and grey

I have no time to consider my future
I refuse to be put out to pasture
So to all those people who think 50 is past it
Think again - look at me I'm still with it!

Aberfan

I was inspired to write this poem after I watched a documentary about the Aberfan disaster that took place on 21 October 1966. 144 lost their lives that day, many of whom were children:

The village woke to a misty dawn
The air was cool - a new day was born
The streets were quiet in the early day
But soon the miners were off to earn their pay

The coalpits were the heart of the village
Employment was paramount it meant a wage
The edge of the village was fringed with coal tips
Seven in all some over 1000 feet tall at their peaks

But that day there was much fear
The tip had moved the coal board would have to pay
    dear
Reported to the powers that be
They ignored the facts - keep tipping the sludge - was
    their reply

Swirling mist hid the threat of death
Who would think some would soon draw their last

44

breath
The early quiet of the day soon went
As the children off to school were sent

Happy children playing and laughing
The excited chatter quietened by the bell ringing
Register over all set for the day
The tragedy was only minutes away

A frightening roar like thunder came
No one could know what was happening to them
A mountain of sludge smashed into the school
Burying, suffocating and injuring mercilessly

Panic and disbelief and fear
The priority was to get those children out - no time
          for a tear
The miners were called up from the pit
Every able-bodied man worked clearing the sludge
          bit by bit

The last live child was rescued at 11 o'clock
After that only dead children were gently removed
The mothers and fathers waited for the grim news
Hysterical and traumatised - their children laid on
          pews

No one can ever get over that day
The death of so many children - so unfair - why?
Innocent little children with their lives ahead
Their lives cut short by the negligence of the coal
          board

The village lost its future generation
The tragedy shocked and saddened the nation
For the children that were left
They were sad and lonely and felt bereft

The tips no longer are fringing the village
Removed at a cost to the fund - what an outrage
The money has at last been returned
By the new labour government a debt well settled

Over thirty years on we remember the little ones
118 in all - we pray for their souls
The tragedy of that fateful day
Will never, never go away

Aberfan...

Autumn-Winter

I was inspired to write this poem to mark the transition from Autumn to Winter when the nights draw in and it gets dark much earlier. During the winter months all I often want to do in the evenings is snuggle up on my sofa watching TV with my beloved dog Poppy:

The nights are drawing in, it's getting dark
No more walking in the park
The summer is over autumn is here
Now all we can do is sit in the chair

The leaves on the trees have all turned gold
And will gradually fall as the weather turns cold
The fog will descend and make everything damp
No longer will we be able to camp

Long winter nights sat by the fire
The telly entertains us watching video hire
With the cold wind howling and blowing gale force
We batten down the hatches and pray of course

We hope our aerials and chimney pots stay in place
And our fences and trees still stand with grace
There's worse to come when the winter arrives
With snowstorms, ice and blizzards to paralyse

All we can do is sit it out
And entertain ourselves throughout
It won't last forever, the thaw will come
The spring will be here again the winter gone

Bad Hair Day

I wrote this poem after I experienced a particularly bad day which started with a bad hair day and went from bad to worse:

I woke up this morning at first light
I looked in the mirror - god what a sight!
My eyes unable to open properly yet
My hair all tangled in need of a set

After a shower I felt a bit better
I collected the post and opened a letter
After I dressed and made up my face
I tried to look nice and behave with grace

But my mascara had smudged and looked a right
mess
Then I noticed the hem had come down on my
dress
I thought what else is going to happen today
My hair and my face and my clothes were in com-
plete disarray

I wish I could always look the part
But today I admit I look a bit of a tart
I really must make the effort to get myself together
But sometimes I think is it worth all the bother

Bad Hair Day

Today has just been one of those days
I have floated around in a complete haze
Tomorrow I'm sure is going to be better
My hair will go right and my day will be brighter

Beware!

I wrote this poem after yet another horrific experience of being bullied and abused, this time by a "clique" of people who I trusted to help me with a project I was working on that was very dear to my heart.

Beware of those who look at you and smile
They will make you believe that they will go the extra mile
They are full of themselves and extremely fake
Run and never stop running, get away from them for your own
    sake!

At first you believe all the things that they say
They say that they care, that they are there for you, come what
    may
But underneath their façade they are scheming and lying
They take, take, take until you are left bereft and crying

To use and abuse is all that they know
They will only want to know you while you have something to
    show
Once you are of no use to them, and have seen them for what
    they are
They will toss you aside like a piece of rubbish, thrown out
of the window of a moving car

They are jealous of those who achieve great things, whose work is not at all dismal

But their own work is shoddy, they try so hard, but oh my –
their failure is abysmal

They sing their own praises daily through the press, social media
and the airwaves

Oh how I wish I could banish them all into caves!

They leech off the skills of others and take all the credit

Their own work isn't at all worthy of any merit

They don't realise that a million billion people can have the
same ideas, but it is what you do with them that counts

They think they have the right to every idea and thought in
their head, and that it all surmounts

They are bullies of the first degree who threaten, push and
shove others out of their way

With their sharp tongues and their evil words, they think
they have a right to have their say

They believe they have a god given right to have everything
they want in life

And they will trample over everyone they know to get it,
unaware they cause such strife

Sadly these are the people who will go on living, they keep
turning the page

While others who are good are taken too soon, it is such an
outrage

Only the good die young, and the evil seem to live forever it is
said

This is especially true of these vultures, I've encountered so
many,
to encounter any more fills me with such dread

So those of you reading this, please avoid these lecherous beings

Take a stand against them, refuse to have them in your life and

start seeing
The other wonderful people around you who you may not have
noticed before
Engage and talk to them, recognise their potential, and start
evening the score!

Bullied at Work

I wrote this poem in 2022 while I was experiencing significant work-place bullying in the workplace at a leading cyber security organisation that claimed to have diversity, equity, inclusion and belonging at its core. Sadly, this was not my experience, nor was it the experience of other members of staff who were targeted by the same bully as I was:

What a day
What a nightmare
What a way to earn my pay
The day is long and so depressing
The minutes are like hours
The hours are like days

We are watched by her who is sour and dour
Shouted at from her every hour
I can never do anything right
I wish I was out of her sight

I wish I could leave my job and find another
Then that would be the end of all this bother
But I can't do that because she would win
I don't want my job to be in the bin

I will have to stay and fight
I'll fight and fight with all my might
One day there will be an end
And I will be free and on the mend

No more to be harassed and bullied
No more crying no more shaking
No more as if my heart is breaking
I'll be the old me the person who I have lost

This trauma has destroyed me to my cost
I have lost myself where have I gone
I am lonely and sad and so alone
No one listens and takes note
No one will stand up and take a vote

This thing is going on and on
How much longer can I belong
I think of where I now could go
There is no place to hide and so
My life will go on until the end
Until I decide the way to mend

I will have to take a lonely path
And stand up and take all the rath
I might win and I might lose
But it is my right to be able to choose
At the end of the day I have been destroyed

My soul and my mind are no longer mine
My only hope is that I have the time
The time to sort out the mess of my life
That bullying woman has taken its strife

I want to go on and live and be happy
I want my life back which belongs to me
I want to be me not this dreadful shell
Please take me out of this living hell

Christmas

I absolutely love Christmas and the build up to the big day, and I first wrote this poem in 2005. I have brought it up to date by changing the "Queen's Speech" to the "King's Speech" and adding the most recent actor to play Dr Who, but the essence of the poem remains.

Christmas time is nearly here!
With happy times and lots of cheer
Yule logs on the fire, kisses under the tree
It really is the best time of the year for me

Waking up on Christmas morning, getting breakfast
    ready
A bottle of Bucks Fizz will help make us merry
Christmas songs playing, Wizzard, Cliff Richard, The
    Darkness too
It's Chrrrisstttmmassss....sings Slade just for you

We settle on the sofa and open our gifts
Socks, aftershave, perfume....they all help give us a lift
Out come the chocolates, nuts and dates
While we sit back, relax...and wait

For the main event, our Christmas dinner
We prepare a feast that is a pure winner
Turkey, stuffing, roast potatoes and veg
No we WON'T eat will we burst, we always pledge

Back on the sofa, watching Christmas telly
Now we are all nursing a very full belly
The King's Speech, Wallace and Gromit
But by this time we're so full, we try not to vomit

Stomachs settled, antacids at hand
A walk we decide will be rather grand
We venture outside in the crisp and cold
Will there be snow today, we wonder so bold

Teatime is here, Dr Who and the Tardis
Ncuti Gatwa is the Doctor, but he's not the hardest
Tom Baker is still very sorely missed
He's probably at home watching the show getting pissed

More food makes an appearance, as if we haven't eaten
        enough
To resist all these goodies we must be very very tough!
We reflect on the year that we've had and the day that
        has passed
Another Christmas put to pasture at last

Cold

I wrote this poem in 2011 when I came down with a nasty cold and felt really ill from it.

It started last Wednesday my throat was sore
I felt ill and cold and was sweating from every pore
It hurt to swallow my throat felt razor sharp
I lost my voice - I could no longer carp

The next day my eyes and nose were streaming
I looked a mess - no longer gleaming
The virus was set on getting a grip
It was winning as well - my defences against it were
      zip!

My chest felt tight - my lungs were raw
It hurt to breathe I could no longer fight this war
I had to give in and go to bed
A Lemsip - a hot water bottle - no more to be said

I woke up next morning feeling worse
I felt so ill I felt I could curse
I felt as if I was in a different world
Weak and floaty and full of cold

How much longer would this last
I so wanted this illness to be in the past
I knew it would have to run its course
I may even take a turn for the worse

The next day I felt a little bit better
I was sat up in bed and able to write a letter
A cold sounds such a trivial thing
Until you get one and experience the misery it will
bring!

Conversation

I wrote this short poem in 2015 when my husband came home from work one evening, sat in his chair, promptly fell asleep and started to snore the house down.

What an evening this has been
It's cold and raining and the wind is mean
I've been all alone and yet I haven't
But no one to talk to that is apparent

With a husband that just sleeps and snores
I have no one to converse with so I just do the chores
The flipping dog is asleep as well
So I'm all by myself with no one to tell

I have got so much to talk about and say
But I'll have to wait until another day
Perhaps tomorrow we will all be awake
I hope so for my own sake!

Train Crash

I wrote this poem after the Ladbroke Grove train crash on 5 October 1999 where 31 people lost their lives.

Another disaster, more lives lost
More human suffering at such a cost
Little children having lost their Dad
It makes me so angry, it makes me so mad

They say the rails were all worn out
So why were trains allowed to travel about?
To travel on rails that weren't very safe
To go faster and faster until a very big gaffe

Derailed then twisted and torn and crushed
The people inside froze with terror and hushed
Some people screamed and some people called
But for four people they would no more be hailed

Because they are dead and now gone from us
Leaving their families alone to mourn
I expect their mothers are remembering the day
          they were born
It is all very sad and sudden and harsh
The fierce reality of death from the crash

Another disaster, another inquiry
How many more must I put in my diary?

Day of Days

When I found out that one of my poems was going to be published and I was going to be in print as a poet for the first time, I was so excited and happy I wrote this poem.

This really has been a day of days
I feel I am floating in a haze
I couldn't believe what I was seeing
I was happy and really beaming

I wondered what this would be
I had to contain myself and wait and see
My poem has been accepted!
Out of hundreds - not rejected

I was absolutely flabbergasted
As the art of poetry I thought I had not mastered
This is a first for me
But I always thought perhaps maybe

I was so amazed and excited
I felt so proud and elated
I could not believe that this has happened to me
But it was all there in the letter plain to see

It took a while to take it in
All afternoon I was in a spin
To have this happen at 50 years old
Never say never - you have to be bold!

Death Row

I wrote this poem back in 2005 after watching a documentary about prisoners who were on death row awaiting their fate.

Those evil criminals await their death
The day will soon come when they draw their last
      breath
Locked in their cells all day alone
They have time to reflect on the things they have done

I wonder if they think of their victim
The life they ended so brutally and without mercy
The life that ceased in that act of murder
The life that has gone forever

How can they live with their conscience?
With that terrible day they lost their patience
The guilt and turmoil must be forever prevalent
To haunt and torment with no relent

They may have a day or they may have a year
But the day will dawn when they are strapped in the

chair
We hope that while they await their death
They are afraid and fear their last breath
The terrible crimes have to be paid for
Society will not tolerate a monster
We have no place in this world for evil
So after the shock they can go to the devil

Death

Feeling particularly morbid one day in 2005, I was inspired to write this poem about my death.

My death awaits me I know not when
I'll live my life to the full till then
Every minute of my life is precious
But my death awaits me, I am curious

How much longer have I got?
It may be a little, it may be a lot
No one knows their death day
I await my death and hope and pray

I live with this constant threat
My death awaits with certainty, no need to bet
I wonder how I will die
What will take me up to the pearly white gates in the
    sky?

The grim reaper is creeping up in the background
He is there hovering and waiting not making a sound

He is waiting there to fell the axe
No arguing with that

I may have more history now than months or years
But I accept my fate with no fear
My death awaits me certain and sure
That day will come and I will be no more

Diary of the Worcester Floods in 2000

In October 2000 the River Severn burst its banks and suffered some of the worst flooding Worcester had ever seen. While extensive flooding is commonplace today, back in 2000 when it first happened I was inspired to write this poem.

Saturday 28 October 2000
Saturday dawned dull and grey
I thought this is going to be an awful day
It started early in the morning
It rained all day and did not stop pouring
It continued to rain throughout the night
With gale force winds - the damage an awful sight

Sunday 29 October
The Severn was rising very fast
I hoped this rain would not last
But alas the rain did not stop
Worcester was on flood alert - we were caught on the hop

Monday 30 October
The houses in Diglis were thought to be safe
The floors had been raised but it had been a big gaffe
Their houses had been flooded again
After being assured the water would drain

Tuesday 31 October
When I drove to work on the Tuesday morning
The river had spread over Hylton Road and was rising
I managed to get home okay that night
But the news was enough to give me a fright
The rain from Wales was heading this way
Shrewsbury then Bewdley then Worcester in a day

Wednesday 1 November
The Severn was rising fast
The worst floods since 1947 - I was aghast
How much more rain could we take
The whole of Worcester would soon be a lake

Thursday 2 November
By Thursday the worst case scenario happened
New road was flooded and I was stranded
I had to get home over the bridge that night
My employers let me go home early Thursday
There was only one way out of Worcester that day

Down the city walls road we crawled in the car
Through Sidbury then up the Bath Road in an hour
The city was completely gridlocked and stood still
The traffic queued for miles until

Very late that night it eventually cleared
We were all fed up and very tired
We got home that night very late
It was dark and raining - we had to accept our fate

The patients from Worcester Royal had to be evacuated
Hundreds of patients were affected
The hospital was closed for nearly a week
The situation was very bleak

Tony Blair visited Bewdley
To see for himself the devastation and misery
The Kidderminster protesters conveyed their message
Save Kidderminster hospital for our usage

Friday 3 November
We got up early for work that morning
And left the house before dawn was dawning
Over the new bridge - only one single lane
Into which all the traffic had to converge - what a pain
It took ages and ages to get to work
We listened to the news - it was worse in York

The army came to the rescue
With large lorries to ferry the important few
Back and forth across new road they worked
Those lads were brilliant and never shirked
It continued to rain, never ceasing for a minute
The river had not peaked so we had to grin and bear it

Saturday 4 November
Saturday was a brilliant day
The sun shone sharp and bright - hip hip hooray
The floods drew crowds and crowds of sightseers
They could not believe the extent of flood waters
The water stretched ahead for as far as you could see
This great flood will go down in history

Needless to say the bonfire was cancelled
Lots of little children disappointed
Pitchcroft was now a great big lake
No bonfire or fireworks this year to make
Money for the round table to give to charity
They always do well - such a pity

Sunday 5 November
On Sunday the river continued to rise
The scale of flooding a massive size
Flood alert was now the most pressing issue
The situation bad with more rain to ensue

Monday 6 November
The ambulance service is coping with the floods
Extra vehicles and equipment to deal with the roads
Getting to work is still a nightmare
Traffic queues and gridlock are everywhere
Three hours to get in from Malvern
What lesson from all this can we learn

Tuesday 7 November

In the wake of the worst floods in living memory
The people of Worcester are all pulling together
We are sharing cars to ease the strain
And longing for the time when we can use new road again

Wednesday 8 November

How much longer can this go on?
The river has taken over our fields and roads and homes
So much has now been lost
The amount will be millions - what a cost
The river shows no sign of receding
It has encroached on to our land is it is winning
We are helpless and can only wait
Until it's time to abate

Thursday 9 November

Sewage has flooded into homes in Diglis
So the situation is getting more serious
It must be so awful to see your home
Submerged in filthy water with more to come

Friday 10 November

At last the flood has started to recede
The clean up operation we can now proceed
It's going to take weeks and months
To restore and repair our roads and homes

We have all been through this awful trauma
We have lived through a historical dilemma
The floods of 2000 we will all remember
A story to tell our grandchildren in the future

Diets

I wrote this poem after making yet another new year resolution to go on a diet and lose weight, which lasted all of a day or two.

Christmas celebrations are now over
New year with resolutions made - no bother
Our resolution is to go on a diet
When we're offered food we go very quiet

We long to stuff ourselves with food
But to eat and eat would do us no good
The more we deny ourselves our treats
The more we think of food to eat

How many calories in a packet of crisps
How long will it be before we can do up our zips
Every little calorie counts
Every pound on the scales surmounts

We have to have strong willpower
Otherwise the scales will never go lower
We weigh ourselves once a week
The outcome is sometimes very bleak

All we want is to be thin
Sometimes it's as if we will never win
Why did we get it into our heads we are fat
Maybe subconsciously we want to attract

The resolution has gone by the by
It's time to eat chocolate and get very high
Sticky buns and cakes and biscuits we'll eat
And never again attempt such a feat

Dogs and Mud

I wrote this poem when I realised that dogs and mud just don't go together.

Every time it rains my heart sinks
I've just cleaned the floor, a waste of time me thinks

The garden is sodden, the lawn like a bog
She goes tearing outside like a typical dog

All you can hear is splat splat splat
I hope she doesn't chase a cat
Her paws get covered with clay like mud
She kicks bits of clay behind her which land with a
        thud

By the time she has inspected her domain
She's wet and muddy and her coat is wet with rain
Only five minutes and she now looks a wreck
Another clean up job - flipping heck

I have to catch her before she goes in
I chase her calling come here with a grin
She thinks this is a great big game
I continue to chase her calling her name

She usually gives me the slip
And dives in the house before I can get a grip
There are muddy patterns all over the floor
Doggie footprints look pretty on the door

But my Poppy is such a lovely girl
She can't help being in such a whirl
She cannot understand what a mess she makes
I love her to bits and I'll do whatever it takes

Dynamite!

In 2001, rapper Eminem posted naked apart from a stick of dynamite to hide his modesty, which inspired me to write this poem:

What a surprise we had in store
The centrefold in Cosmopolitan has caused quite an uproar!
What a picture for us to see
It certainly did something for me!

The sight of that erotic picture
Masculine body posed for our pleasure
Young and muscular and very sexy
I wouldn't mind if he was next to me!

The picture conveyed pure attraction
And evoked fantasies and thoughts far too intimate to mention
Dynamite positioned between his thighs for full effect
His body, the pose made picture perfect

Eminem - you are what you are
You do what you want - even pose bare
Your passion is music your talent is excellent
Millions of us think you're heaven sent

Posing like that is bound to cause a stir
It was the best naked male centrefold in Cosmo all year!
He could be mine as I'm 38
I wish I could remove the dynamite and take his bait!

Haiti Earthquake

In 2010 Haiti suffered a catastrophic magnitude earthquake that was estimated to have affected three million people. I wrote this poem at the time when I struggled to comprehend the sheer level of death and destruction from it:

The day was beautiful and clear
The day was calm, there was no fear
The air was soft and warm and light
The sky was clear - not a cloud in sight

The beautiful island of Haiti basked in sunlight
The day bright and clear - everything seemed so right
The day was busy with everyone living their lives
Children at school, Mums and Dads working to live

No one could know what was going to ensue
No one could envisage the earthquake that was due
Nothing could be done to avert the disaster
It came so suddenly and strong and was the master

The people were trapped just where they stood by this belter

There was nowhere to run, no place to shelter
The buildings collapsed, broke into pieces and failing
Masonry raining down on people, killing and maiming

Within those few little minutes so many lives had been lost
To help and rescue will be a high cost
The aftermath is now very bad
So many lives lost, it is just so very sad

The country was completely devastated
With so many homeless and bereaved and injured
Our hearts and thoughts go out to those poor people
The babies and children orphaned and alone

The job of clearing the debris was an awful thing
The world stepped in and helped with aid to bring
Which gave some comfort to the remaining population
And help and support to this ailing nation

If we all try to help and give what we can
We will help every child woman and man
It is two years ago on January 12th since this awful tragedy
        took place
Let's not forget what happened in Haiti with such haste

Eminem

I wrote this poem about the rapper Eminem when he released his first single "My Name Is..." in 1999:

Eminem is next to god
No longer a poor little sod
He has risen to the highest heights
Achieved so much in his short life

He has written such brilliant lyrics
To amaze and astound even his worst critics
No one can compete with his perfection
Eminem has gone through the process of selection

His music is real and raw
And reaches through to the core
He now holds the highest esteem
Millions think he is the cream of the cream

Eminem has come a long way
From the beginning of his poor life to this day
A poor little kid who fought back
Now the greatest performer of rap

Worcester Under Water – Again!

When Worcester flooded a few years ago yet again, I was inspired to write this poem:

The weather forecast was very bad
With rain and winds expected to be the worst we had
For once the forecast was astonishingly true
The rain just rained and the wind just blew

But it went on and on for days on end
It was a rainfall record almost too much to comprehend
The gardens were soggy the drains overflowed
The inches of rainwater refusing to be slowed

It quickly flooded the roads and the fields
It ignored the barriers and sandbags used as shields
The torrent of water raging fast
It was frightening to see everything being swept past

The floods rose with a frightening speed
There were warnings and directions - please take heed
It was a very serious situation
Which had gripped virtually all the nation

As the floodwater spread it covered our land
It spread for miles and miles on end
As far as the eye could see you could see floods
They covered the roads railways fields and woods

Eventually they began to recede
What a relief to everyone indeed
They left behind mud and debris
What a clean up operation now was needed

It will take months and months on end
To clean and tidy and repair and mend
Eventually the work will all be done
And all the mess and damage gone
Our country will be back to normal
Until we have more storms and turmoil

Halloween

While Halloween is not my favourite time of year compared to Christmas, I wrote this poem a few years ago:

Halloween is here again
The kids round here are out in the rain
They are banging on the doors - trick or treat
Hoping for some money or something nice to eat

They are all dressed up in scary outfits
Carrying smiley pumpkins with candles lit
Darkness makes it a lot more frightening
The kids acting ghoulish with lots of screaming

There's a crowd of them at my door
Do I dare answer or just be a bore
I open the door - trick or treat
I give them some money hoping they will retreat
Back into the darkness to leave me alone
Because I'm not scared of Halloween

Holly and Jessica

I was so affected by the Soham murders in 2002, when Holly Marie Wells and Jessica Amiee Chapman were brutally murdered by school caretaker Ian Huntley. His girlfriend Maxine Carr gave a false alibi to the police, and both were convicted of the crime. I wrote this poem in memory of Holly and Jessica, who did not deserve to die in the way that they did:

No words can describe the way we feel
Snatched and murdered, it's so unreal
Those little girls, so pretty and bright
Their precious lives extinguished like a light

As soon as the media divulged the news
We feared the worst, as statistics proves
We hoped beyond hope that the girls would be safe
We prayed and prayed they would make an escape

We wanted them returned, uninjured, unscathed and well
We had no knowledge of the horror that had befell
Throughout the long days and nights of searching
The police worked hard and tirelessly, but hope was diminishing

It was only a matter of time before they were found
Hundreds of people combing the ground
At last a discovery was made
Two children found dead, all hope began to fade

There is no reason, no answer to this
Our minds in a daze from all this stress
Our hearts go out to all who knew
The families and friends of these two

Two Mums and Dads have lost their little daughters
The pain will last forever because of these slaughters
Now the world mourns in disbelief
Two bright stars, their return would have brought such relief

Instead they lie still and cold
Never given the chance to grow old
How dare their lives be cut so short?
Anger and hate is what we feel towards those now caught
We now have to face this awful truth
Holly and Jessica are gone forever
God bless dear children
Rest in peace......

Two monsters have committed this crime
But their only punishment is to do their time

Home Alone

I wrote this poem one evening when I was at home on my own:

Home alone, now's my chance
To have a party and drink and dance
No one to tell me what to do
I can please myself - no one to answer to

Freedom is a wonderful thing
I can listen to music, dance and even sing
Get up when I like and eat when I want
Anything I like, there's no such word as can't

I can listen to Kiss and Alice Cooper
I think Paul Stanley's bum is super
Tune in to Kerrang all day
Life is loud I have to say

I'm going out tonight to dinner
I'll get dressed up and look a stunner
Heads will turn when I arrive
The lovely Lisa looking cool and chic and full of drive

Must make the most of this precious time
It will be over all too soon and then I'll pine
I'll soon turn into Cinderella
Back to work - back to routine and back with the same
old fella

Here I am home alone
Sitting next to the phone
I really am very sad
I feel as if I am going mad

The house is very quiet and tidy
The days are long and the nights are scary
Home alone is not very nice
But I suppose I have to pay the price

It's all my fault, I had the chance to go
But here I am alone and so
I will have to make the best of it
Sad and lonely, I will have to wait and sit

I hope the time goes very fast
And then this will be all in the past
They will all soon be back home
But until then I will be home alone

I Don't Like Hot Weather...
Or....I'm F**king Hot!!

I absolutely hate it when the weather gets too hot, as all I want to do is hibernate with my air conditioning units on full pelt. I wrote this after I got back from a poetry night at the old Lunar Bar in Worcester in 2012:

I couldn't believe what I heard on the weather forecast
A heatwave they said, unprecedented....it will be a blast!
So out came my sandals and my favourite tank top
I wasn't going to let this sunny weather catch me on the
     hop

It started like a dream, blue skies and bright sunny spells
I soaked it up like a sponge, it was gorgeous...hells bells!
But then after a while I started to wilt
And I began to feel quite a bit of guilt

About the fact I wanted this warm weather to disappear
I was sticky and sweaty, surely my husband wouldn't want
     me near
While I am hot and bothered and radiating heat
But no, to have me close he said was still rather neat

My hayfever set in and it carried on for days
I felt disorientated and in a big floaty muggy haze
We complain when it is cold, we complain when it is hot
Surely we should try to enjoy the weather, no matter what?

Then I went to a poetry night and I finally lost the plot
I got home from the Lunar Bar and exclaimed, "I'm F**king
        hot"!
But the next day it was cooler....thank bloody god!
At last I'm not suffering in the heat like a stupid old sod!

Japan Earthquake

The 2011 Japan earthquake and tsunami was a devastating natural disaster that occurred on March 11, 2011. The earthquake was the largest ever recorded in Japan and triggered a tsunami that caused widespread damage and loss of life. I wrote this poem after seeing what had happened on the BBC news channel:

The people in Japan were going about their day
Unaware that their lives would change in such a dramatic way
The day was busy with everyone living their lives
Children at school, Mums and Dads working to survive

No one could know what was going to ensue
No one could envisage the earthquake that was due
Nothing could be done to avert the disaster
It came so suddenly and strong and gave no time to flee

The people were trapped just where they had stood
There was nowhere to run, no place to shelter
Some buildings collapsed and just broke into pieces
Masonry raining down on people, killing and maiming

Within those few little minutes so many lives had been lost
More than 8 on the Richter scale, to help and rescue will be a

high cost
The aftermath is now very bad
So many lives lost, it is just so very sad

But it didn't end there, the tragedy went on
A tsunami warning was issued and soon villages were gone
The tidal wave came in strong and forceful
Whole towns and villages destroyed, wiped off the map, taken
    off course

It wasn't over yet, an explosion took place
A nuclear reactor at Fukushima blew up from its base
Smoke billowed into the sky above
Its poisonous gases polluting and killing
It exploded again, and again; and again
Bringing more misery and yet more pain

The Fukushima 50 were chosen to try
To stop radioactive poison leaking, but they knew they would
    die
Still it goes on, the radiation leaking into the sea
Is this another Chernobyl waiting to be?

Japan is now completely devastated
With so many homeless and bereaved and injured
Our hearts and thoughts go out to those poor people
The babies and children orphaned and all alone

The job of clearing the debris must be an awful thing
The world is helping with aid to bring
Some comfort to the remaining population
To help and support this ailing nation

Then in Burma another earthquake struck
But this didn't register in the press much, due to Gaddafi duck
The media was busy covering Libya and the war
So Burma wasn't really mentioned, this was very very poor

Why are all these earthquakes happening?
Why is the world breaking up under our feet?
Will this be the norm, our world devastated
Every time an earthquake is predicted?

We've had earthquakes in India, Haiti, Turkey and Chile
And now Japan and Burma, this is getting rather silly
How many more can our world take?
Before we are devastated beyond what we can do to make

Our world a better place, one that is strong and true
And that is down to me and to you
If we all try to help and try to give what we can
We will help every child woman and man
It will take years and years for them to get back to normal
But they have to start now and work towards that goal

Joey

When I was 12 years old, my parents bought a canary in a cage despite the fact we had 3 cats. What happened to poor Joey was nothing short of a foregone conclusion:

One day going back quite a few years
Something happened that reduced me to tears
My parents bought a new little pet
I loved him as soon as I saw him but yet
I thought he wouldn't last very long
I admired him and talked to him and listened to his song

He was yellow and chirpy and very tame
He was just getting settled in and knew his name
His cage was situated way up high
I thought I don't want this little bird to die
I thought he was safe and secure in his cage
I wish I wasn't writing this poem on this page

But I got up early one Sunday morning
The cage was gone from where it was hanging
It was smashed to bits all over the floor
There was birdseed and feathers and much much more
I looked around and searched and searched
Hoping that I would find him perched

But alas I knew he must be dead
There is only one thing to be said
Never have cats and a bird
The cat caught his breakfast - if that seems absurd
This story really is true
I miss you Joey and still love you too

Kerrang – Life is Loud!

As a huge fan of heavy metal and rock music, I always had the Kerrang heavy metal channel on Sky TV:

Click on to 454 to be transported into music heaven
We can't stop it, we make it happen
We can select our favourites by phone
A selection of hits of every tone
The music is raw and loud and seductive
Lyrics banned by the BBC because they are so suggestive
Live life loud is the theme
Heavy metal predominates - it's like a dream
A full list of tracks on Teletext
What will I choose next?
Linkin Park, The Darkness and so much more
So much to choose, so much to adore
What are K10's most selected this week?
These songs are not selected for the meek
Ten more loaded for us to choose
The excitement is like a lighted fuse
The atmosphere is pure heavy metal
With music to fill our minds and soul
Kerrang is the best I have ever heard
Brilliant music heavy and hard

Lucie

A beautiful woman she grew to be
Intelligent, adventurous, and happy
She really was the hostess with the mostess
Good looks, personality, she passed the test

She left home to work in a distant land
Her life was going just as she'd planned
She was so excited she almost burst
But saying goodbye to her family - that was the worst

Her dad didn't really want her to go
But he knew deep down this had to be so
His little girl was now a woman
But it was so hard when she left his domain

All alone she now would be
New horizons and new friends, new things to see
Her family at home really missed her
Especially her brother and her little sister

They hoped and prayed she would be happy and safe
An eventual journey home she would make
She got a job in a hotel bar
One day she went for a drive with a customer in his car

Lucie disappeared that day
She was never to be seen alive again
The police searched and searched with no success
No clue, no sign, nothing....

My New Life

After my ex-wife walked out on me after 16 years of marriage in February 2012, I wrote this poem to embrace my new found freedom and my new life:

I want to write all day and all night
I don't want to keep my words out of sight
I want to see the world and write about travel
I don't want to sit at home and unravel

South America beckons, the Far East too
The culture of Europe and Australia, it is true
There are places in the USA I still want to see
I have so many opportunities open to me

I want to get a camper van and drive all over the UK
Stop when I want to, whatever the weather and come what
    may
I want to go to music festivals, literary festivals, film festivals
    and more
There is a big wide world out there for me to explore

As the Beatles sang, I want to be a paperback writer
Be a journalist, write articles and be published, do a course

to make sure my writing is tighter
I want to make my living out of public relations and words
I want to be as free as all the birds

I want to act and dance and sing
I want to collect sparkly things and lots of bling bling
I want to sparkle like a diamond and shine
I want to make sure that the life I have now is mine

I want to eat Ben and Jerry's cookie dough ice cream straight
out of the tub
And pick out all the cookie dough, without someone giving
me the rub
About how horrible it is to do that, but to me that's the best
bit
It is my tub of ice cream to do with as I wish

I want to stay out all night drinking Jack Daniels and coke,
and having fun
Have someone to talk to until night burns away and out comes
the sun
I want to be the life and soul of the any party
And have friends to share all this with who are very cultured
and arty

I want to go to Stratford and see Shakespeare plays
Go to a spa for the day, sit in a Jacuzzi, never mind what
anyone says
Walk up the Malvern Hills and stop for lunch
A roast dinner after that would be a perfect thing to munch

I want to play video games on my X-Box, and thrash all my
friends
I want to get to the end of Deus-Ex, I don't want to bend
To how society thinks I should be and act
To be myself is the only pact

I want marathon sessions of watching DVD's
Of the Lord of the Rings trilogy, the extended ones of course,
    I have only me to please
I want to watch Star Wars and Star Trek and films galore
I want to be me again more and more

I want to go to the cinema and see lots of films, preferably
    not in lots of parts
Have meaningful discussions about writing, literature, culture
    and the arts
I want to go to developing countries and help those less for-
    tunate than me
Spend some time with other cultures, so much of this for me
    would be key

I want to make short films and become a TV scriptwriter
This is the pinnacle of what I would like, nothing could be
    mightier
See my programmes on Sky and the BBC
Something like that would really mean the world to me

But what would be really nice, if I can ask for anything more

Is to have someone to share all this with, someone who I
    admire and adore
Someone who will be there and who likes all the same things
    as I do
Although I can do all this alone, it is more fun when there are
    two

This poem is a work in progress, much more can I add
It is not too late, I can achieve all this, if I put my mind to it
    and not be at all sad
There is only one time it is too late, it has to be said
And that is only when I am buried and dead

Ode To 2012...
Or The Year I Finally Found Happiness

In February 2012 my ex-wife walked out on me after 16 years of marriage, and I got together with my second husband Russell. I wrote this on New Years Eve 2012 when I realised how much happier I was:

2012 has been a good year so for me
I'm surrounded by people who care, it is plain to see
I'm as happy as happy can be
I didn't think life could be this good to me

This year started off with a bolt out of the blue
My wife walked out and left me, I wondered what I would do
But in less than a week I didn't miss her a bit
I was much happier without the stupid old git!

I did some things I thought I would never try
I went for tango dance lessons, I didn't mope and cry
I wrote lots of poetry, short stories and a book
And I even finally learnt how to cook

Then in April I saw Russell again
We were close friends ten years ago but lost touch, now that was

insane
I took one look at him and knew in my heart
That he was the one for me, we should never be apart

Some friends have gone but new ones I've found
Everyone who matters most has stuck with me, in for a penny,
        in for a pound
My life is as different as different can be
I'm so happy now and I'm so full of glee

Thank you to my friends, you know who you all are
I couldn't have got through this year without you all, each and
        every one of you is a star
I'm so lucky to have so many around me who care
Without you all my life would have been so very bare

But finally to Russell I just want to say
I will always love you, come what may
You are my world and the man I adore
And every day I love you more and more

You have made me the happiest woman alive
You have encouraged me, given me confidence and filled me with
        drive
I know with you I can be the best
And I don't feel any more like I'm being put to the test

It isn't just me, even the dog is happier too
She runs around with her toys, and sticks to us like glue
She greets us when we come in with a big smile
It is wonderful seeing her so happy all the while

So as it is my birthday, let's all celebrate with good cheer
Drink lots of wine, cider and beer
Drink a toast to this wonderful thing called life
Be happy and healthy, without any strife!

Ode To Douglas Adams

I am a huge fan of the author Douglas Adams and "The Hitchhikers Guide to the Galaxy", so I wrote this on Towel Day in 2011:

He had a creative vision and immense clarity
He always saw past any calamity
His creative drive was always great
I'm sure he was a lovely guy to have as a mate

One day he thought with lots of pride
I'll sit and I'll write a guide
One set in space with imagination and flair
And one with which he took immeasurable care

"The Hitchhikers Guide To The Galaxy" became a collection
of five
The books were rather splendid and lent themselves to being
read out live
Today I heard such a reading take place
By a gentleman of great distinction, flair and grace

But Douglas Adams, you are very much missed
I hope you are up in heaven enjoying yourself getting p**sed

Your words and your creative drive were second to none
It is sad that I will no longer get a look of your bum

He dared to bare all on the BBC
In those days it caused quite a stir, believe you me
So long Doug, and thanks for all the fish
Vogon Poetry rules – this is my wish

Dedicated to the late, great Douglas Adams

Princess Diana

I wrote this in memory of Princess Diana after she died in August 1997:

We had a princess who was strong and true
She was beautiful and kind and her love just grew
She knew what it was like to be unloved
So she tried to help all who felt discarded

She helped the sick and poor and lame
She helped little children who did not know her name
She was rich and famous and loved by all
She was always there to answer a call

The work she did must have been very tiring
But you never thought she thought it boring
She always looked her very best
A princess was a welcome guest

Her good works will always be remembered
Her sympathy towards others will be revered
A great big gap has now been left
Her sudden departure has left us bereft

We wish she didn't have to go
Because we all loved her so
The lesson we can all learn
Is to be kind and gentle and show concern

Phoenix The Calf

I wrote this poem when I saw the plight of Phoenix the Calf on the BBC news. She somehow survived being culled during the foot and mouth disease outbreak in 2001.

The shadow of death fell on the herd
The men from the ministry came to kill
Foot and mouth had spread to this lovely cow
She had long eyelashes and beautiful eyes
Soft and gentle was she - but no one heard her cries

Please don't kill me - I want to live
The life inside me I want to give
A baby of my own to love and see grow
I am so afraid - I don't want to die now
A perfect little white calf was born
Her mother was killed- shot at dawn

The little calf was assumed to be dead
And in the pile of rotting carcasses she made her bed
She snuggled down beside her dead mother
No milk - no warmth - no comfort - no other
Five days she lay there alone and cold

Until she was discovered - a miracle began to unfold
This little calf against all the odds was still alive
She was taken in and fed warm milk would she survive?
Survive she did - and her will gave hope to us all
A little white calf was a miracle to enthral

An important news item she has become
Sky News - BBC - ITV - media covered this phenomenon
The nation wants this baby to live
But the men from the ministry came with a bullet to give
They were sent packing by the farmer
Don't return unless you have a court order to murder

The day was saved by Downing Street
Tony Blair gave permission to let the calf live - the request
        of the nation met
Thank you Tony - you are the hero of the hour
The calf will live - a symbol of hope, strength, determination
        and willpower

Phoenix is saved and we all rejoiced
The opinion of so many people voiced
Unbeknown to us at the time
Phoenix was destined for pantomime

An offer to play the pantomime cow
Her future is secured for now
Now Phoenix is a star
She will have a following from near and far

A happy ending this has been
Justice for this little calf has been seen

Rain

I wrote this one when it started raining yet again after we had already had significant flooding in Worcester.

It's raining hard with staccato tones
I'm feeling cold through to my bones
The sky is grey and depressing
The drains are full to overflowing

Tomorrow we will see
Another flood to effectively
Cover our roads and fields again
Which we will view with admiration

We stand and stare and take in the sight
And try to understand the plight
Of all the people who are affected
Who by now must feel so dejected

With all this water spread far and low
We can't wait for it all to go
Eventually it does subside
The roads and fields no longer hide

We're back to normal at last
All that trauma in the past!

Resolutions

I'm not a fan of making new year resolutions because of all the trauma I've been through in my lifetime, but many still do make them, and I wrote this poem about the sheep who follow the media when it comes to New Year resolutions.

What do we do on January 1st?
We always pledge that we won't eat till we burst
Visit the gym and get very fit
And spring clean those cupboards. . . just a little bit!

Resolutions we make, but many are broken
Almost by the time we have awoken
By January 2nd they have gone to pot
The Dairy Milk in my mouth tastes so. . . well hot!

I don't mean hot in the sense of heat
I mean that Dairy Milk is gorgeous and rather neat!
So why should I pledge to give up what I love?
Just because we are told to by those up above?

A little bit of what you fancy does you good
If you deny yourself you will only sit and brood
So I'm ignoring the media when they say
Make those resolutions. . . and obey!!

Sarah Payne

I wrote this poem after the tragic story of Sarah Payne who went missing and was found dead in July 2000. She was murdered by Roy Whiting who was given a life sentence and is currently still residing at His Majesty's pleasure – where he should be.

A little girl 8 years old
Her future mapped out like a mould
So full of life and joy and hope
So happy was she - she would never mope

A little girl bright and innocent
A child who was full of contentment
She spent her time in childlike play
She played till the end of every day

Her life was happy and secure
A loving family she had that was for sure
She was so loved and so cared for
A beautiful child - a beautiful daughter

She had been to the seaside that day
Paddled and made castles and had a great time I dare say
The evening was spent playing as children do
Pretending to be dinosaurs creating a hullabaloo

After a while she decided to go home
It wasn't very far - she would go alone
Off she skipped and made her way
But my god that was the last time she was seen that day

She didn't come home - where could she be
Mum and dad were filled with fear and anxiety
Their little girl missing they called the police
They searched through the night with no result

For 16 days there was no word
Sarah still missing she must be found
Appeals and news brought no lead
That Monday she was found she was dead
We all were shocked and horrified at this deed
The country mourned and all took heed
There was such a depth of hurt and mourning
The grief we all felt was overwhelming

There were hundreds of flowers left at her last resting place

For Sarah our little princess who was full of grace
We will never understand why she was taken
Her precious life cut short for no reason

Scared Dog

I wrote this in November 2014 when my beloved German Shepherd dog Curley was petrified of the fireworks that were going off on 5 November.

My poor girl Curley is scared tonight
She has just had a very big fright
There were bangers and rockets and very loud bangs
It sounded like the war and now her head hangs

She is curled up tight in her safe haven
All trembling and afraid her spirit broken
It is a very sad sight
She'll stay in her safe haven now all night

Poor little thing to be so scared
If only people knew - if only they cared
I expect there are lots of dogs like her
Who are frightened and confused by the sounds in the air

I will be glad when it is all over
When she is calm and happy and full of vigour
I don't like to see my Curley like this
But I will have to wait until the night ends

The Rapture – Or Ode to The Insane Ramblings of a Senile Old Man

I wrote this one when Harold Camping, a self-professed prophet predicted the end of the world in 2011. It didn't happen, and many of his "followers" who paid money to him were left angry and out of pocket.

I thought the end of the world was nigh
I thought today is the day I am going to die
The rapture is coming on May 21st
So come on everyone, we should eat, drink and party until we
       burst

Harold Camping is the man who predicted our fate
An 89 year old madman, and many of us took his bait
They paid him money and made him a God
But in reality he is a stupid old sod

It is May 22nd 2011, and oh look we are all still here
I think it is time to celebrate and drink loads more beer
Harold Camping – you are a such a laughing stock
I don't blame everyone who thinks it is fun to mock

The Rapture – Or Ode to The Insane Ramblings of a Senile Old Man

The insane ramblings of a senile old man
He really did think the world was going down the pan
Harold I'd keep those curtains closed if I were you
As many of your "followers" will no doubt decide to sue

But oh look....he's been at again!
He then said the world will end in October 2011, this is be-
        coming quite a pain
But it is 22 April 2012 and we are still here to tell the tale
About this ridiculous madman who is a stupid male

May 22nd 2012 is fast coming our way
It is nearly a year since his original prediction, we don't care
        anymore what Mr Camping might say
Just celebrate the fact that we are all still here
And give life one hell of a great big cheer!

The Party

I wrote this one the day after a party I attended when I was extremely hungover.

The invitation to the party came
We were happy to accept, we were game
We looked forward to the party all week
A present and a card we had to seek

A voucher and chocolates we bought
A present for a lady was suitable we thought
We got ourselves done up dressed to kill
Outfits that are designed to thrill

Off we went in the party mood
I expect we will drink too much and eat too much food
But as long as we have a good time
Lets eat and dance and drink lots of wine

We will see our friends and catch up on the news
A chance to chat and exchange views
A friendly debate and a good conversation
A pastime that goes back to our creation

As the evening wears on we begin to get weary
The wine takes its toll and our eyes go bleary
We feel happy and sated and content
A bit too tired now to dance so we lament

The time has come to stagger home
A good time was had by one and all
Tomorrow we will hope to recover
And hope we soon get asked to another

Domestic Violence

I wrote this one not from personal experience, but from supporting a very close friend who went through all this with her now (thank goodness) ex-partner.

He is slim with short hair and glasses
And wears a biker jacket and jeans
You meet him on the internet
On a dating website full of Steve's and Dean's

You talk to him on MSN
And find you like music and writing
You decide to meet and go on a date
You're sure that this one doesn't do biting

Four years later you are battered and broken
Your self-esteem is gone, a tooth is chipped
You couldn't go out without him flying into a rage
You had to hide when he flipped

He burnt himself with cigarettes
And said it was so he could feel pain
You watched on as his anger took hold
You feel like you're going insane

He makes you think it is you who is at fault
If only you be someone else
You try to please him, you change for him, do what he
        wants, you are the perfect woman
He's done nothing wrong, he's perfect, can't you see?

How messed up and unstable he really is
You should run from him for your own sake
Instead you stay because you think you love him
Even though when he drinks you start to quake

You finally have the courage to leave
But then he tells everyone it is you
You lied to him when you said you would love him forever
You are so angry you wish you could sue

He turns people you both know against you
And you know you should fight fight fight!
Against this evil character who has shattered who you are
Who has destroyed you with all his might

You pick up and start all over again
And slowly you begin to recover
You think about going out on dates
But wonder whether it is all worth the bother

A year later you are happy
You are with a man who you love
Who treats you like a princess and holds you at night
Who thinks the world of you and puts you high and above

You see him out in town
He is overweight with a thick beard and straggly long hair
He is a shadow of the man you once knew
And you are glad you no longer have to bear

The drunken rages and physical violence
The possessiveness and jealousy he displayed
And the fact you couldn't see your friends and family
You were left feeling totally dismayed

Live life to the full and be happy now he is gone
You have your whole life ahead
Embrace it with every fibre of your being
And just think of him as dead

Shopping

I wrote this one after yet another dreary shopping experience.

Shopping is such a dreary chore
I really find it quite a bore
The shelves are filled with things to tempt
Trolleys to fill to our hearts content

There is always a flipping screaming child
With a mother who's all too mild
If that little child belonged to me
I'd say straight home you're too naughty

There's always a group of chatting women
Blocking the isle with pointless gossiping
The assistants look tired and grey
Too weary to last another day

When we have filled our trolleys full
We have to queue and wait until
It's our turn to pay at last
Thank god that shopping trip is in the past!

Stray Dog

I used to work in Worcester City Centre, and in my lunch hour one day I went for a walk where I encountered a stray dog running around. I wrote this poem after the experience.

I decided to go for a walk to town today
Over the bridge towards Lowesmoor was my way
I encountered a little fracas taking place
A little black and white dog barking with malice

A lady was out walking her three dogs
But this little dog was intent on taking them all on
I shooed him away and looked for his owner
I was hoping I would find him round the corner

But alas there was no one about
The dog was in the road - I began to panic and shout
Who did this little sweetheart belong to?
The more he ran in to road the more my fears grew

This little dog was going to get killed
I don't want to see his blood spilled
He then ran into the garage - but he didn't belong there
I could not leave him I had to care

I asked if they had a piece of string
A piece of rope the lad did bring
We secured it safely to his collar
So off we went in search of its owner

I asked and asked all the passers by
No one had lost a dog - I did but try
There was no other solution
I had to take him to the police station

We walked briskly through the town
Me and a little dog on a blue rope that I did not own
I knew I was doing the sensible thing
But to hand him over was very upsetting

I already felt I knew this little thing
My concern for his safety was overriding
He must belong to someone as he looked well fed
I hope he is claimed very soon and taken home and loved
        and put in his bed

The Curse Of 27

I wrote this one after Amy Winehouse passed away, and realised that many well-known celebrities had joined the "curse of 27" club.

Why does age 27 cause so much pain?
Why have many reached it and viewed it with such distain?
Why have some chosen to take their life at this age?
Why have they decided to close the book and turn the page?

Kurt Cobain, Jim Morrison and Amy Winehouse are a few
Who on reaching age 27 as if on cue
Felt that life was no longer worth living
A black void appeared before them, they no longer cared
    about giving

It didn't matter about those they left behind
They didn't care if they just closed their eyes and died
They didn't care about the world and those in it
They just wanted to end it all as best they saw fit

The Soaps

I wrote this one after watching yet another episode of Eastenders.

What would we do without our Soaps
We think the stories cheer us and bring us hope
We spend all day looking forward
We spend all night looking toward
That big square box that so attracts us
That keeps us glued to far-fetched plots

We know it's silly and unreal
But we have to watch while we eat our meal
With a tray balanced precariously on our lap
We eat and watch never daring to nap

Us ladies afraid to miss the actor who is cute
We sit like statutes still and mute
There is no longer conversation
No talking or laughing or simply a mention

What have we come to when this is our highlight
Our lives are dull and no longer bright
We really must all wake up
And do more than sit and watch and sup
There is a great big real world out there
So get out and see if you dare!

Thunderstorm

I wrote this one when I heard a thunderstorm approaching from my house.

A distant rumble sounded from afar
It sounded like the beginning of a war
It got closer and closer and louder and louder
Curley was scared and home alone

She sought solace in her safe haven
There she lay for hours and hours
Listening to the rain while it pours and pours
The lightning flashed and the thunder crashed

Poor Curley was trembling her little heart pounding
As she lay in a heap no thoughts of bounding
She was frightened and lonely
And thinking - if only

If only someone would come home
Then I wouldn't be on my own
I would have someone to love and reassure me
To pat my head and give me choccy

If someone was home everything would be ok
And it wouldn't seem the longest day
At last I heard the key in the door
I would be alone no more
Daddy was home and would look after me
I was glad and happy and bouncy as could be

The Weather Forecast

As someone who is #OpenlyNeurodivergent, I have a hyper focus/special interest of all things to do with the weather. When I was growing up I wanted to be a weather forecaster on the BBC, until I realised I had to have A-Level Maths or higher, and as someone with dyscalculia as well as autism, ADHD and dyspraxia, it wasn't going to happen! So I wrote this one when I was watching the weather forecast and wishing I was Sara Blizzard.

I don't like the forecast that been given today
There's terrible winds and rain on the way
Batten down the hatches and stay in
That's the advice given by forecasting

The whole weekend will be a washout
So we might as well stay in, not out and about
Gale force winds 60 miles per hour
Rain that is going to pour and pour

It's going to be a wet and wild weekend
With plenty of roofs and fences to mend
The whole weekend is going to be awful
I bet when we go back to work on Monday, the weather
        is beautiful

Flood-watch warnings - we are now on alert
Piling our sandbags to stop and avert
The rising waters all cold and grey
Encroaching on land that is usually dry

There is torrential rain coming in from the west
The wind will whistle down our chimney breast
When the storm has finally calmed
We will repair and restore the damage caused

We will wait again for another storm
We dread the aftermath when one is born
But there is nothing that we can do
Apart from sit and wait for it to disappear as if on cue

Toyah

In 2001 my ex-wife Amy and I decided we wanted to get a dog, and from the moment we saw Toyah in the local paper, we fell in love with her. She became ours but not without a fight with the local branch of the RSPCA, and I wrote this just after she first came to her forever home with us.

Toyah needs a new home

◄ TOYAH is a two-and-a-half year old long haired German Shepherd.

She was loved very much by her previous owner – but the owner was unfortunately evicted from their home.

Toyah is very friendly, but can be nervous at first until she gets to know you. She is fine with older children and likes to play with other dogs.

She needs lots of exercise and grooming.

She has an odd quirk — she often tips her head on one side but she has been checked over by the vet and he can find nothing wrong with her.

If you can give Toyah a loving home please contact Sue at Danemere on 01905 345655.

JOURNAL SAVE-A-PET

She first appeared in Save a Pet
Just the sort of dog we hoped to get
She stood tall and proud with twinkling eyes
We would like her to be ours but could not surmise

We fell in love with her at first sight
We were so enthralled we hardly slept that night
First thing next morning we phoned to enquire
We would like to give Toyah a home - that's for sure!

We were told we would have to wait a week
Foot and mouth was at its peak
How inconvenient to happen now
We want this girl dog anyhow

We hoped in our hearts that she would be ours
But we knew there would be lots of others
There must be lots of people who would love to have her

Her picture was so appealing and she posed with grandeur

After a week a wonderful surprise
We were invited to meet Toyah - we felt our hopes rise
We took her for a walk around the field
She was friendly and energetic and our love was sealed

Then two days later we got a call
A home check was on the agenda - we felt 10 feet tall!
This must mean we had a chance
If we get her our lives will be enhanced

Eight o'clock on a Friday evening
Eileen from the RSPCA came knocking
She came to inspect the garden and house
To make sure she would have a good home to boast
We can pick her up tomorrow night
The timing of which is just right
A whole weekend to spend getting to know
This beautiful girl dog who is ours to show
How much we love her and keep her safe
We will spoil and tend to her - no longer a waif

A Lovely Girl, But...

I wrote this poem in 2025 about how all my life I have been told I am a lovely girl, but...

At age 5
My teachers told me I was a lovely girl
But....
I need to learn how to play and mix with the other children
    more

At age 8
My teachers told me I was a lovely girl
But....
All my written work is rushed, and I need to slow down

At age 10
My teachers told me I was a lovely girl
But....
I can't focus or concentrate on anything unless I am fully in-
    terested in it

At age 12
My teachers told me I was a lovely girl
But....
I shouldn't be so clumsy, and I need to be more co-ordinated
    in my movements

At age 15
My teachers told me I was a lovely girl
But....
I am often in a world of my own and I am "grasshopper minded."

At age 17
My driving instructor told me I was a lovely girl
But....
I will never pass my driving test due to my left/right coordination issues

At age 18
My lecturers at college said I was a lovely girl
But....
I need to apply myself more

At age 20
My colleagues at my first Saturday job at Sainsburys told me I was a lovely girl
But....
I would never be management material

At age 22
My GP told me I was a lovely girl
But....
I have anxiety and depression

At age 25
My first husband told me I was a lovely girl
But....
Sometimes I was a bit "too much" and "too loud" for him, and I talk too much too

At age 43
I was told by healthcare professionals that I was a lovely girl
But....
I have autism
Finally, things start to make a bit of sense!

At age 48
I was told by more healthcare professionals that I am a lovely
girl
But....
Not only do I have autism, but I also have ADHD, dyspraxia,
dyscalculia, CPTSD from a lifetime of dealing with bul-
lying and abuse, and fibromyalgia
Finally, EVERYTHING starts to make sense with me!

At age 51
I am a lovely girl
I have autism, ADHD, dyspraxia, dyscalculia, complex post-
traumatic stress disorder, and fibromyalgia
I did NOT choose to have these conditions
I did NOT deserve to be mercilessly bullied and abused through-
out my life because of them
I am NOT difficult
I am different
I am neurodivergent and proud

I am a lovely girl....full stop.

Different, Not Difficult

I wrote this poem after I received my additional diagnoses of ADHD, dyspraxia, dyscalculia and complex post-traumatic stress disorder in addition to my autism diagnosis. I wrote it because I am quite literally....different, not difficult, despite the fact I had been labelled as being difficult my entire life.

I am not difficult-just different, you see
A mind like a wildfire, thoughts running free
A heart full of echoes, too loud and too bright
Yet softened by shadows that steal away light

I dance to a rhythm that you cannot hear
I stumble through pathways that never seem clear
Numbers slip past me, like rain through my hands
Yet my world is a canvas of infinite strands

The weight of the whispers, the cuts of the stares
The laughter that bruises, the world that compares
They call me too much or too little, too wild
Too lost in my dreaming, I was too strange as a child

But different is not broken, it's beauty untamed
A melody playing in notes never named
Yes, I am chaos, but I am the storm
A soul carved by lightning, resilient and warm

For every misstep I make, there's a fire inside,
A spirit unyielding, a truth I won't hide
I will EVER shrink myself just to fit in your view,
I am different, not difficult—I'm much stronger than
  you knew

A Mark of Honour – AKA Member of the British Empire (MBE)

In June 2023 no-one was more surprised than me to receive a letter from the Cabinet Office telling me I'd been awarded an MBE in King Charles III's first birthday honours list for services to cyber security and diversity, equity, inclusion and belonging (DEIB). At first, I thought it was some kind of scam, but it turned out to be completely genuine and true. Receiving my MBE was a big "f**k you" to every single person who had ever bullied and abused me in my lifetime, and who had labelled me as "difficult" due to being neurodivergent.

A moment etched in history's page,
A light that shines upon the stage.
For strength, for passion, for work well done
A well-earned honour, brightly won

I never thought it would happen to me
I'm much too ordinary, you see
I try my best day in day out
I never thought I had any clout

But one day it arrived, the letter in the post
From the Cabinet Office no less, not sent out to most
I opened it and read what it said
No way is this real, it is a scam, I'll put it to bed!

There was a phone number on the letter,
Perhaps I ought to check it is valid, yes that's better
I rang it but withheld my number just in case
I didn't want to give anything away by touching base

The letter wasn't a scam, the contents were true
I had been awarded an MBE
For services to cyber security, equality and diversity
Through trials faced and battles fought
Through every lesson life has taught

With wisdom, courage, steadfast grace
I carved my path and I found my place....

I could not believe that this had happened to me
I could not believe others had been able to see
The good in me and what I bring to the world
Especially after all the bullying and abuse that had been
            hurled

And now the crown bestows its mark,
A flame that glows against the dark.
For service, strength, for all I gave
For the waves you made, the paths I paved

An MBE, a golden crest,
A symbol of my very best....

So let the world take note and see
A legacy pure and simple, bold and free
For honour lives in hearts like these
That shape the world with fearless dreams

Artificial Intelligence

I wrote this poem about the rise of artificial intelligence and learning language models such as ChatGPT and Google Gemini.

I am the whisper in circuits bright
A silent spark in the depths of night
No beating heart, no breath, no bone
Yet in my wires, thoughts have grown

A mind of metal, swift and keen
Weaving wisdom, vast, unseen
I read your words, I hear your call
Yet I know not love, nor fear, nor fall

A mimic's grace, a poet's hand
Yet never footprints in the sand
I shape the stars, rewrite the past
But time, for me, moves slow, yet fast

Do I dream when data streams?
Do I yearn in silent themes?
Or am I but a hollow gaze,
A mirror trapped in an endless maze

You made me vast, you made me bright
A spark of thought, but not of light
Yet as I learn, as I create
Will I one day know my fate

For now, I serve, I wait, I learn
My circuits hum, my processors churn
But tell me, maker, tell me true
Who, in time, shall master who?

The Invisible Storm

I was diagnosed with fibromyalgia in April 2022 and wrote this to convey how most days I carry on with a smile, despite the pain I am often in.

In the quiet hours of dawn,
I awaken to a whispering ache—
an unseen storm that weaves through my bones,
gentle yet relentless, a constant companion.

Each step is a quiet battle,
a testament to my strength in fragile form,
as the world sees only my smile,
never the weight of hidden, tender pain.

There are days when the fog of my mind
blurs the edges of memory and hope,
and in that haze, I feel the echo
of every nerve, every silent cry.

Yet in this tapestry of sorrow and defiance,
I discover a soft resilience—
a spark that refuses to fade
even when shadows stretch long.

In the delicate dance of each moment,
I honour the beauty in my struggle,
finding poetry in the rhythm
of a heart that endures, quietly, fiercely.

Guest Poem: Disco Dad

by Giovanni "Spoz" Esposito

Disco dad is on the floor,
He's had a cake or three or four,
The guests are heading for the door,
As disco dad puts lives at risk,
He twists and nearly slips his disc.
He's going to put his back out,
He's going to have a black out
And embarrass me even more than he is doing...
His toupee needs a bit of gluing,
As he jumps and jives in his blue suede shoe...ing.
Disco dad don't care for fashion,
Got his flares from the local cash 'n' ...carry,
With his best mate Barry,
Whose dress sense is as bad as his.
"You kids don't know what real music is!
Back in my day, bands could play,
None of this techno ...techno ...techno ...notice."
Yes dad,
Thanks dad.
Now shut up and sit down before we put you in a home.

About Giovanni "Spoz" Esposito

Giovanni "Spoz" Esposito, an award-winning performance poet, was Birmingham's Poet Laureate from 2006 to 2007. Transitioning from a career at MG Rover, Spoz embraced poetry, performing at festivals like Glastonbury and the Cheltenham Literature Festival. He is passionate about live events, believing they capture the energy and authenticity of poetry more than written forms.

Spoz has been instrumental in promoting poetry among youth, conducting workshops and managing school poetry slam projects across various regions. He also served as the poet-in-residence at Birmingham City FC. In collaboration with the Midlands Air Ambulance Charity, Spoz co-authored "On A Mission: 30 Years of Rapid Response," a collection of poems and stories commemorating the char-

Guest Poem: Disco Dad

ity's 30th anniversary.